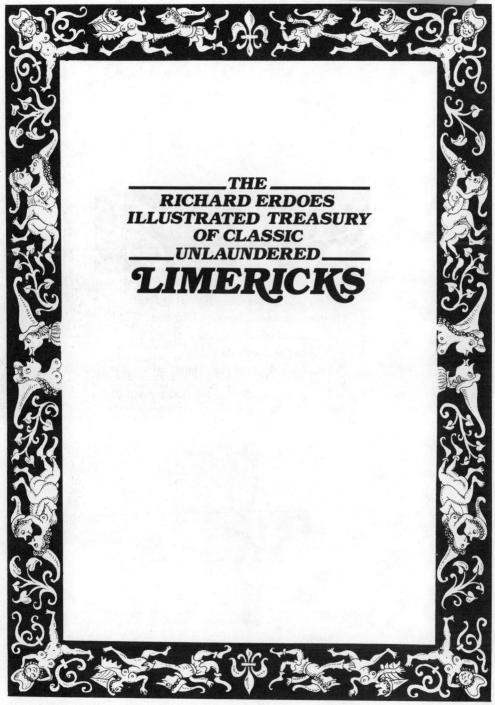

THE
RICHARD ERDOES
ILLUSTRATED TREASURY
OF CLASSIC
UNLAUNDERED
LIMERICKS

Tell me, what does the lecherous Erdoes?
He does just what a bee or a bird does.
        It would make your hair curl
        What he does with a girl,
Because him does the same thing that her does!

— Isaac Asimov

THE
RICHARD ERDOES
ILLUSTRATED TREASURY
OF CLASSIC
UNLAUNDERED
LIMERICKS

INTRODUCTION BY ISAAC ASIMOV

balsam press

Selections in this book have been reprinted from
A Grossery of Limericks by Isaac Asimov and John Ciardi,
by permission of W. W. Norton & Co., copyright © 1981
by Isaac Asimov and John Ciardi; from *Limericks Too Gross,*
or *Two Dozen Dirty Stanzas, A Duel Between Isaac Asimov
and John Ciardi,* by permission of W. W. Norton & Co.,
copyright © 1978 by W. W. Norton & Co.: and from *Lecherous
Limericks* by Isaac Asimov. Used with permission of the publisher
Walker and Company
Copyright © 1975 by Isaac Asimov.

ISBN 0–917439–01–5

Distributed by Kampmann & Company
          9 East 40th Street
          New York, New York 10016

Library of Congress Cataloging in Publication Data

Erdoes, Richard.
   The Richard Erdoes illustrated treasury of classic
unlaundered limericks.

   1. Limericks.   2. Bawdy poetry.   I. Title.
PN6231.L5E7   1984   808.81'7   84-11014
ISBN 0-917439-01-5

Designed by Allan Mogel
Edited by Barbara Krohn

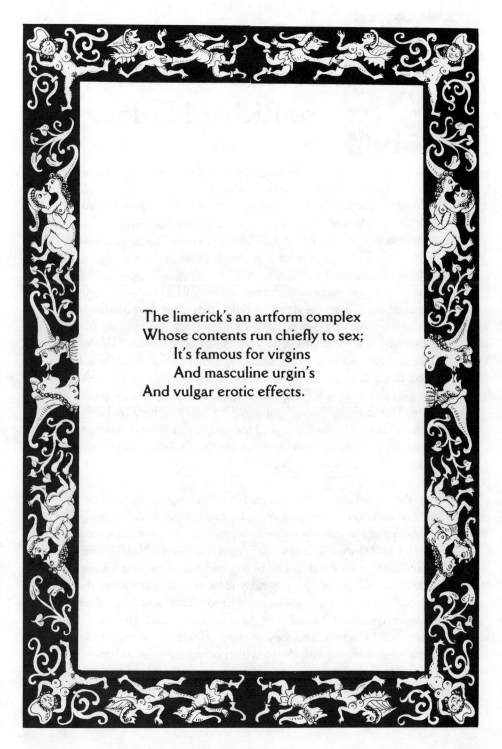

The limerick's an artform complex
Whose contents run chiefly to sex;
    It's famous for virgins
    And masculine urgin's
And vulgar erotic effects.

PREFACE
by Richard Erdoes

Sex is what makes the world go round. It makes lions roar, glowworms glow, and birds sing. It induces sober-minded men to learn the tango and impels women to paint their lips and do strange things to their hair. Without sex, painters would not paint and poets would not compose poems. As to the military, to quote General George Patton, "Soldiers who don't f*** don't fight." The urge to mate is almost as strong as the urge to eat and drink—often stronger.

Therefore, it's not surprising that matters sexual have always occupied the minds of men since the dawn of time. Ever since *homo sapiens* acquired the art of writing, sex occupied a focal point in literature. Mighty epics dealt with the dalliances of gods, kings, and heroes. There was great Zeus disguised as a swan, seducing Leda; in the shape of a bull, ravishing Europa; in the form of a cloud, raining gold into Danae's lap; sampling gay love by carrying off Ganymede while masquerading as an eagle. The "Song of Songs" got into the Old Testament by being declared a symbol of heavenly love. Heavenly indeed! And the Romans learned their bedside manners by studying Ovid's *Art of Love*, and they thrived on gossip describing orgies inside the palaces of Caligula and Heliogabalus.

From the beginning, certain aspects of human sexuality struck people as being tremendously amusing. We can suspect that Cro-Magnon men and women guffawed while they related their crude amorous anecdotes inside dark and dripping caves. The Aurignacian and Magdalenian female faceless figurines with gravid bellies and huge drooping breasts and buttocks—were they really just fertility idols, or was there some shaggy fellow fondling them, smiling with some apropos remarks about their exaggerated physical attributes? The Athenians chuckled while watching Aristophanes' *Lysistrata*, and they showed off with pride their red- and black-painted drinking vessels on which outrageous sexual goings-on were lovingly depicted. Chaste matrons, in the hope of conceiving, prayed to the image of Priapus with his mighty, oversized phallus. Did they not tell jokes afterward?

The Romans were titillated by the elegant, humorously impudent verses of Martial and Juvenal, and medieval Englishmen enjoyed the earthy passages in Chaucer's *Canterbury Tales*. To Martin Luther, we owe this little gem:

Every week twice
Is sure no vice.
A hundred and four per year,
That's very nice.

A lifestyle one could grow old with!

Renaissance Italians had Boccaccio and his *Decameron*, Frenchmen had Rabelais, while Englishmen of the Restoration period recited the Earl of Rochester's truly depraved poems. And the Elizabethans, oh, those Elizabethans! Merry old England in the seventeenth and eighteenth centuries was a golden age of whimsical erotic poetry. Not for nothing was the Great Bard of Avon also known as "the Great Bawd." To Robert Burns, we owe a whole spate of unabashed lyrics celebrating the thing good Scotchmen had beneath their bellies so white. In America, good old Ben Franklin wrote a treatise about making "Bowel Winds" sweet-smelling, and also an advice to young swains to make love to old, experienced women.

The Victorian Age tried to suppress the lust for life, except when this enjoyment was clandestinely practiced—but repression only bred volcanic eruptions.

Mark Twain's *1601* was privately printed with the help of a Protestant clergyman. Balzac's *Droll Stories* were secretly enjoyed by dim candlelight by sweet young things in English "Ladies' Academies." And poor Queen Victoria lived to learn of the amorous adventures of her son, naughty Bertie, the Prince of Wales, who later ascended to the throne as King Edward VII. At the same time, her own relations with her Scottish Gillie caused much comment. You can't keep a good thing down!

Limericks were written as early as the sixteenth century, but attained their true, definite form only during the first years of Queen Victoria's reign. But of course! And those earliest Victorian ditties were also the

There once were two ladies of Birmingham,
And this is a scandal concerning 'em.
    They lifted the frock
    And tickled the cock
Of the Bishop engaged in confirming 'em.

raunchiest. The one about the two ladies of Birmingham is an example.

Around 1900, and later, limericks became more elegant and sophisticated—but perhaps they also lost some of their primal quality. Some of the foremost poet laureates, like Algernon Swinburne and Robert Service, presumably contributed their mite. Yet many of the great masters of bawdy limericks were loath to acknowledge authorship, which might cost them a poet laureateship, while those who claimed the honor sometimes didn't write them at all. G. Legman, possibly the greatest authority on the subject, tells of several men claiming to have penned a certain famous limerick, one of them a German who couldn't even speak enough English to write the cover letter.

The great poet Goethe invented a sort of German unlaundered limerick, the so-called *Wirtin Verse*. One of these dealt with an unlucky smith, endowed with a square *membrum virile* which, in great fury, he hammered into the required cylindrical shape.

As to the authorship of the limericks in this collection, most of them come from sources which can generally be defined as folklore, the authorship being anonymous, as a general rule. In the cases where we know the poet, we have, of course, clearly given the attribution. G. Legman, in the erudite introduction to his *The Limerick, 1700 Examples With Notes, Variants, and Index*, gives his reason for this:

> ...who are the authors of bawdy limericks? It is understood that most limericks entertain only their authors, and, whatever attempts may be made to circulate them, never achieve folklore status at all. But what of the others, that everyone knows—who writes them? Some of the original authors, when the form was new, and classics were being cast in the hot mould of Victorian anti-clericalism...include Swinburne, to whom what must be Limerick No. 1 in any collection has always been ascribed, the charmingly normal idyll in extravagant rhyme, as to the young couple of Aberystwyth, 'who united the organs they kissed with,' moving on finally—in lay-analytic terms—from oral to genital stage at last:

There was a young girl of Aberystwyth
Who took grain to the mill to get grist with.
The miller's son, Jack,
Laid her flat on her back,
And united the organs they pissed with.
— Attributed to Swinburne

Another known limerick author from Swinburne's time and circle was
Dante Gabriel Rosetti (who obviously had to write them, if only to get the
"languid love of lillies" of his published poetry out of his system).

And the editors of the late, lamented magazine, *Eros*, echo Legman's classification of limericks as being either folklore, or certainly cousins of folklore:

> Hardly an educated man is now alive who does not treasure in his memory at least one limerick, proper or improper. The chances are that he did not read it in a book or magazine. Rather, he acquired it by hearsay: it was passed on to him by word of mouth, by 'oral tradition.' As such, the limerick is authentic folklore—a vital part of our heritage.

The comment by the *Eros* editors about "the educated man" brings up another curious observation—that in our own century, some of the best limericks came out of Berkeley, Harvard, and Yale. As one connoisseur remarked: "They arise not from the amorphous, unlettered, unwashed multitude, but from amid the educated class." Without doubt, it takes an educated mind to fashion a first-class limerick.

Even such a professorial Puritan as President Wilson managed to compose at least one off-color limerick to which he proudly acknowledged authorship:

> I sat next to the Duchess at tea;
> It was just as I feared it would be:
>   Her rumblings abdominal
>   Were truly phenomenal,
> And everyone thought it was me.

Bawdy limericks are indeed a treasured part of Anglo-Saxon literature and folklore, love-children of serious poesy—as British as the "roast-beef of Old England" and as American as the Stars and Stripes, apple pie, and reverence for motherhood. Enjoy, read and remember, and pass on the flame!

> The limerick packs a laugh anatomical
> Into space that's quite economical.
>   But the good ones I've seen
>   So seldom are clean.
> And the clean ones are seldom so comical.

There was a young lady of Chichester
Who made all the saints in their niches stir.
    One morning at Matins,
    Dressed only in satins,
She made the Bishop of Chichester's britches stir.

NTRODUCTION
by Isaac Asimov

I have written five collections of original limericks (some of which un-chaste five-liners are included in this volume), and so it seemed natural to the publisher to include an introduction of my own to this book.

Once I saw the illustrations, I was absolutely delighted to have my introduction appear, for it was clear to me that words expressing the serious and forbidden themes characteristic of the best limericks are in-sufficient. You need visual representation as well; you need to see as well as hear; you need artwork.

Richard Erdoes, who is responsible for the art, hits just the right note in my opinion. He sharpens and intensifies both the humor and the un-laundered nature of the limericks, producing a felicitous marriage (or, if you prefer, a passionate liaison) of text and drawing.

But what is a limerick? It is a stylized verse form and is as meticulously structured as a sonnet. Consider the limitations as far as form alone is concerned:

(1) It must consist of five lines: no more, no less.

(2) The rhyme scheme must be a,a,b,b,a. That is, the first, second, and fifth lines must rhyme. The third and fourth lines must rhyme also, but they must have a different rhyme from that of the first, second, and fifth lines.

(3) The first, second, and fifth lines must consist of three feet each; that is, each must contain three stressed syllables. The third and fourth lines must consist of two. This means there must be thirteen feet to the limerick — no more, no less — distributed among the lines exactly as I have indicated.

(4) The typical foot of the limerick is an anapest. That is, it consists of

two unstressed syllables followed by a stressed one: dih-dih-DAH. All thirteen feet of the limerick can be anapests, but it is quite usual for one or two of the initial feet in the lines to be iambic; that is, to consist of one unstressed syllable followed by a stressed one: dih-DAH.

(5) The rhyme may be masculine, involving a single syllable such as "main" and "plain"; or it may be feminine, using two or even three syllables, such as "measure" and "treasure" or "healthier" and "wealthier." Therefore, the last foot in a line may be dih-dih-DAH, dih-dih-DAH-dih, or even dih-dih-DAH-dih-dih. The two different sets or rhymes in the limerick can be either both masculine, both feminine, or one masculine and one feminine.

With all this in mind, here is the rhythm of a typical limerick:
dih-DAH dih-dih-DAH dih-dih-DAH-dih
dih-dih-DAH dih-dih-DAH dih-dih-DAH-dih
    dih-DAH dih-dih-DAH
    dih-dih-DAH dih-dih-DAH
dih-dih-DAH dih-dih-DAH dih-dih-DAH-dih

If you want to see what this rhythm is in words, here is a limerick (not mine, alas) containing the precise rhythm given above:

There was a young couple named Kelly
Who walked around belly to belly
    Because, in their haste,
    They used library paste
Instead of petroleum jelly.

It is conventional to indent the third and fourth lines, both because they are shorter than the other three and because it is convenient to emphasize that there is a change in rhyme for those two.

What is just as important as the metrical rigidity of the limerick is the nature of the content:

(1) The limerick must represent a complete story, with a beginning, a middle, and an end. This, in itself, is a neat trick, considering that the longest legitimate limerick can only have forty-nine syllables and that it can be as short as thirty-four syllables. The limerick I have quoted above tells the tale of the appalling misfortune that overcame two young lovers and does it completely in thirty-eight syllables.

There was a young couple named Kelly
Who walked around belly to belly
    Because, in their haste,
    They used library paste
Instead of petroleum jelly.

(2) The limerick must be humorous — that is, if it is to be a real limer-ick, and not merely a set of lines that just happen to have the limerick form. For instance, in *The Yoeman of the Guard*, W. S. Gilbert includes a song that begins as follows:

> A man who would woo a fair maid
> Should 'prentice himself to the trade.
>> He should study all day
>> In methodical way
> How to flatter, cajole, and persuade.

As far as rhyme and meter are concerned, this is a perfect limerick — but only as far as those are concerned. It is neither complete nor funny; nor, to do Gilbert justice, was it intended to be, in itself, either complete or funny.

(3) At least part of the humor should be expressed by the cleverness or unexpectedness of the rhymes. Here, for instance, is a classic limerick that startles and delights in its clever rhyme of "Titian" and "Coition."

> As Titian was mixing rose madder,
> His model posed nude on a ladder.
>> Her position to Titian
>> Suggested coition,
> So he swarmed up the ladder and had 'er.

Naturally rhymes of this sort cannot be used in serious poetry because they elicit laughter in themselves and can therefore only be used in comic verse. The limerick is not, and is never intended to be, serious poe-try. In fact, so firmly has the limerick established itself as comic verse, that any poet attempting to write serious poetry in the limerick meter, even if he used only the most somber of rhymes or no rhymes at all, would find it difficult to be taken seriously. The dih-dih-DAH dih-dih-DAH of the lim-erick has swallowed up gravity completely.

(4) The humor should be vulgar and should deal with actions and words that society likes to regard as nonexistent — reproduction, excre-tion, and so on. This is not an absolute requirement and you can, indeed, have "clean" limericks. The following one by The Reverend Charles

As Titian was mixing rose madder,
His model posed nude on a ladder.
 Her position to Titian
 Suggested coition,
So he swarmed up the ladder and had 'er.
    — Carlyle Ferren MacIntyre

Lutwidge Dodgson, better known as "Lewis Carroll", is an example:

There was a young man of Oporta,
Who daily got shorter and shorter.
    The reason, he said,
     Was the hod on his head,
Which was filled with the heaviest mortar.

Clean limericks, however, usually lack flavor, like vanilla ice cream or pound cake. They are perfectly edible, but, to my taste, are tame, flat, and unsatisfying.

The "vulgar" limerick (usually called the "dirty" limerick or, as in this book, the "unlaundered" limerick) has its value because to the humor of rhyme and the challenge of metrical rigidity, it adds the relief of release. You can relax, for the space of some two score syllables, the bonds of social decorum that hold you in thrall most of the time. The sad tale of the couple named Kelly is an example of completely successful vulgarity.

(5) Many limericks end the first line with a proper noun, of either a person or a place. Such proper nouns come in all kinds of sound patterns and give you a starting platform. You then need to find only two rhymes to it. If the proper noun is difficult to rhyme, the limerick becomes an exercise in ingenuity. Here, for instance, is a limerick (not my own) that goes:

A woman who lived in Antigua
Once said to her mate, "What a pig you are!"
    He answered, "My queen,
     Is it manners you mean?
Or do you refer to my figure?"

As written, the rhymes don't look very good. When recited, however, the words can be slurred in such a way that they become excellent — and hilariously unexpected. This makes the limerick satisfactory, for ideally the limerick should be recited, and the written form is merely a guide to minimize forgetfulness. Sometimes, the directions for the spoken version are made explicit in the written version as when the last words of lines two and five in the limerick above are written "pigua" and "figua." This sort of misspelling is permissible, but it should be used very parsimo-

Concerning the bees and the flowers,
In the fields and the gardens and bowers,
  You will note, at a glance,
  That their ways of romance
Bear not much resemblance to ours.

niously. It can be insulting to the reader, and it can degenerate into a cheap snatch at orthographic humor.

(6) Many limericks start off: "There was a young woman of —" (or old man, young man, old woman, and many other variations). Here is a limerick (not mine) of this type:

There was a young lady of Yap
With pimples all over her map.
        But in her interstices
        There lurked a far worse disease
That is commonly known as the clap.

This is complete, vulgar, and it contains one of the cleverest rhymes I have come across: "interstices" and "worst disease." And yet the limerick falls short of perfection because the clever rhyme comes in the third and fourth lines. The laugh comes *there*, and the fifth line verges on the anti-climactic.

Let me stress, though, that the first line of the limerick need *not* be "There was a young woman of —" and the end of the first line need *not* be a proper noun. Let the other requirements be fulfilled, and these first-line "failures" are forgiven and, indeed, are not even noticed.

As I said earlier, limericks should be recited. Well recited, they are funnier than they can possibly be in cold print — but there are precautions you must take:

(1) For heaven's sake, don't recite a limerick unless you are sure you are syllable perfect. If you forget and stop, all value is lost. If you forget and improvise and come out with a syllable too few or too many, the effect is greatly weakened.

(2) In reciting the limerick, emphasize the rhythm and rhyme just a little bit. You're not supposed to do this in reading serious poetry. By proper emphasis, you get across the humorous aspects of the limerick more efficiently. It helps, in this respect, if each line ends at a natural pause, if the words do not "run on" without a break from one line to the next.

(3) I have my own private feeling that a limerick should be occasionally sung, if you have the voice for it. Limericks are an Anglo-American tradition, and so are comic songs, and why not combine the two? My own favorite tune for limericks is the one to which the Gilbertian "A man

It's time to make love. Douse the glim.
The fireflies twinkle and dim.
    The stars lean together
    Like birds of a feather,
And the Loin lies down with the Limb.
        — Attributed to Conrad Aiken

who would woo a fair maid" is sung (may the shade of Sullivan forgive me!). If you don't know the tune, any Gilbert and Sullivan addict will teach it to you.

(4) If you do sing a limerick, don't sing too many of them, for the tune will pall. Indeed, don't recite too many of them at one time, for the whole thing will pall. The most effective limerick is almost always the one you recite first. The funniest in the world will not get more than a snicker if it comes fifth.

I mentioned earlier that the limerick is an Anglo-American tradition. I have no doubt that limericks can be written in almost any language — and, as a matter of fact, the one about the plumber of Leigh will be found further along in this book in French, German, and Latin as well. But I have the feeling that no language other than English can create the limerick as easily, as numerously, or as humorously.

The fact that the form and meter are so rigid means that the story you want to tell must be shuffled a bit, adjusted, molded, shaped. A syllable must be added here and dropped there. The result is that you must be ready at all times with a set of synonyms and substitute phrases.

As it happens, English has the largest vocabulary of any language. It is strongly idiomatic and has an almost anarchically loose spelling and grammar. All this means that English is precisely the kind of triple-jointed language you need for endless adjustment until, finally, it folds up neatly into the five-line, two-rhyme limerick.

The limericks included in this book, let me say at once, are vulgar, and almost all of them are concerned with sex. If you are going to be offended by "dirty" limericks, please put the book down — there is no intention here to offend.

However, there is vulgar and vulgar. A limerick can be merely vulgar without being clever. It can reach for shock value only, be more unpleasant than it has to be, be repellent or even nauseating. Interestingly enough, as Richard Erdoes points out, it is usually the earliest ones — the Victorian limericks — that are the crudest. Some of these are included because no earnest collection of classic limericks would be complete without them, but mostly, the limericks in this collection aim for more wit than vulgarity, and that is what counts.

One last plea —

Don't try to read the book at a sitting. Just read till you feel yourself stop laughing. Then put it aside and try it again after at least a twenty-four-hour rest. The book will seem funnier, and will also last longer that way.

There was a young sailor named Bates
Who did a fandango on skates.
    But a fall on his cutlass
    Rendered him nutless
And practically useless on dates.

here was an old man of
Nantucket
Who kept all his cash in a bucket;
But his daughter named Nan,
Ran away with a man,
And as for the bucket, Nantucket.

Pa followed the pair to Pawtucket
(The man and the girl with the bucket)
And he said to the man,
"You're welcome to Nan,"
But as for the bucket, Pawtucket.

Then the pair followed Pa to Manhasset,
Where he still held the cash as an asset;
And Nan and the man
Stole the money and ran,
And as for the bucket, Manhasset.

A broken-down harlot named Tupps
Was heard to confess in her cups:
    "The height of my folly
    Was fucking a collie —
But I got a nice price for the pups."

 young man with passions
   quite gingery
Tore a hole in his sister's best lingerie.
      He slapped her behind
      And made up his mind
To add incest to insult and injury.

A beach boy who loved to have fun
Kept screwing a girl in the sun.
      While his ass, being bare,
      Cooked to medium rare,
The girl kept exclaiming, "Well done."

Said a certain young maid of Tortuga,
"How I wish I could mate with a cougar.
      The sheer joy of matching
      Would be worth the scratching."
But her friends think she's clearly meshuggah.
                              — Isaac Asimov

There was a young lady from Sparta
Who was a magnificent farter.
    She could fart anything
    From "God Save the King"
To the Beethoven "Moonlight Sonata."

She might give a gavotte for a starter,
Or maybe, "The Christmas Cantata."
　　Then, Boom! from her ass
　　Burst Bach's "B Minor Mass,"
And, in counterpoint, "La Traviata."

There was a young fellow named Hyde
Who fell down a privy and died.
   His unfortunate brother
   Fell down another,
And now they're interred side by side.

A woman who lived in Saint Paul
Had breasts undeniably small.
    Her husband growled, "Dear,
     Why not burn your brassiere?
It's fulfilling no function at all."
      — Isaac Asimov

There was a young girl from Cape Cod
Who thought babies were fashioned by God.
    But t'was not the Almighty
    Who hiked up her nightie —
'Twas Rodger, the lodger, by God!

"Well, I took your advice, Doc," said Knopp,
"Told the wife to get up on top.
    She bounced for an hour,
    Till she ran out of power,
And the kids, who'd grown bored, made us stop."

A guy with a girl in a Fiat
Asked, "Now where on earth is my key at?"
When he started to seek,
She let out a shriek:
"That's not where it's likely to be at!"

here once was a startled young
  Syrian
Who, coming home late, and who peering in
    The window to coo
    To his wife, beheld two
Rather lithe Lebanese disappearin'.
                — John Ciardi

A very smart lady named Cookie
Said, "I like to mix gambling with nookie.
    Before every race
    I go to my place
And curl up with a very good bookie."

Well bugged was a boy named Delpasse
By all of the lads in his class.
    He said, with a yawn,
    "Now the novelty's gone,
It's only a pain in the ass."

There was a young plumber of Leigh
Who was plumbing a girl by the sea.
    She said, "Stop your plumbing,
      There's somebody coming!"
Said the plumber, still plumbing, "It's me!"

I y avait un plombier, Francois,
Qui plombait sa femme dans le Bois.
    Dit-elle, "Arretez!
      J'entends quelqu'un venait."
Dit le plombier, en plombant, "C'est moi."

Prope mare erat tubulator
Qui virginem ingrediebatur.
    Dessine ingressus
    Addivi progressus:
Est mihi inquit tubulator.

Es giebt ein Arbeiter von Tinz,
Er schlaft mit ein Madel von Linz.
    Sie sagt, "Halt sein' plummen,
    Ich hore Mann kommen."
"Jacht, jacht," sagt der Plummer, "Ich binz."

There was a young fellow named Lancelot
Whom his neighbors looked on askance a lot.
    Whenever he'd pass
    A presentable lass,
The front of his pants would advance a lot.

here was a sage hermit named
   Dave
Who kept a dead whore in a cave.
      He said, "I'll admit,
      I'm a bit of a shit,
But think of the money I save."

There was a young fellow from Juilliard
With a penis that measured a full yard.
      The girls whispered and leered
      And most of them cheered,
Whenever he ran through the schoolyard.
                              —Isaac Asimov

In the farm belt, a hooker named Blum,
Who's the favorite floozy of some,
      Takes her teeth out in bed
      To administer head,
And her tricks, they all love it, by gum!

toothsome young starlet
named Smart
Was asked to display oral art.
　　As the price for the role,
　　She complied — met his goal,
And then sank her teeth in the part.

There was a young fellow named Bliss
Whose sex life was strangely amiss.
　　For even with Venus
　　His recalcitrant penis
Would seldom do better than th$_{\text{is}}$.

There was a young man with a hernia
Who said to his doctor, "Goldernia,
　　When carving my middle
　　Be sure not to fiddle
With matters that do not concernia."
　　　　　　　　— Heywood Broun

"For the tenth time, dull Daphnis," said Chloe,
"You have told me my bosom is snowy;
    You have made much fine verse on
    Each part of my person,
Now *do* something — there's a good boy!"

widow who lived in Rangoon
Hung a black-ribboned wreath at her womb.
　　"To remind me," she said
　　"Of my husband, who's dead,
And of what put him into his tomb."

On the talk show last night, Dr. Ellis,
The sex shrink, took two hours to tell us
　　It's all right to enjoy
　　A rosy-cheeked boy
So long as your sheep don't get jealous.
　　　　　　　　　　— John Ciardi

To his bride, said the lynx-eyed detective:
"Can it be that my eyesight's defective?
　　Has your east tit the least bit
　　The best of your west tit?
Or is it a trick of perspective?"

Lisped a limp-wristed cowboy named Ray,
"It's a hell of a place to be gay.
   I must, on these prairies,
   For shortage of fairies,
With the deer and the antelope play."

42

While smooching around in the grasso,
With a comely young lady, Picasso,
   One chilly November,
   Inserted his member.
Now, both cubist and pregnant that lasso!

here was a young fellow
named Perkin,
Whose wife caught him jerking his gherkin;
    She said, "Mr. Perkin,
    Stop jerkin' your gherkin,
You're shirkin' your firkin' you BASTARD!"

There was a young person named Clarence,
Who cabled from Sweden: "Dear Parents:
    Sex-change operation
    Creates new relation.
As Clara, implore your forbearance."
                — John Ciardi

An impoverished young couple named Skeat
Used to bundle to save on the heat.
    But six kids in five years
    Left them in such arrears
That they never again made ends meet.
                — John Ciardi

From the depths of the crypt of St. Giles,
Came a scream that resounded for miles.
 Said the vicar, "Good Gracious!
 Has Father Ignatius
Forgotten the Bishop has piles?"

 team playing baseball in Dallas
Called the umpire a shit out of malice.
    While this worthy had fits,
    The team made eight hits
And a girl in the bleachers named Alice.

How bitter was Joseph's existence
When he found that his girlfriend's insistence
    Meant that he'd have to wed her
    Before he could bed her.
She was simply a pièce de résistance.
                    — Isaac Asimov

I once had the wife of a Dean
Seven times while the Dean was out ski'in'.
    She remarked, with some gaiety,
    "Not bad for the laiety,
Though the Bishop once managed thirteen."

An Argentine gaucho named Bruno
Once said, "There is one thing I do know:
    A woman is fine
    And a sheep is divine,
But a llama is numero uno!"

Shipwrecked off an island near Bali,
A salt found a mermaid to dally.
    It bloodied the sailor
    And ended in failure:
Her vagina, impossibly scaly.

lady with features cherubic
Was famed for her area pubic.
        When they asked her its size,
        She replied in surprise,
"Are you speaking of square feet or cubic?"

A sweetly developed young creature
Developed a crush on a teacher,
        Who developed a lump
        That developed a bump
That is now her most prominent feature.
                        — John Ciardi

There was a young man from Madras
Whose balls were constructed of brass.
        They jangled together
        In inclement weather
And lightning shot out of his ass.

When the Bishop of Solomon's Diocese
Was stricken with elephantiasis,
    The public beheld
    His balls as they swelled,
By paying exorbitant priocese.

here once was a smooth-
talking Druid
Whose manner of living was luid.
  He'd engage Druid lasses
  In small talk — no passes,
But the first thing they knew they'd been scruid.
                                        — John Ciardi

A thrifty young fellow of Shoreham
Made brown paper trousers and woreham;
  He looked nice and neat
  Till he bent in the street
To pick up a pin; then he toreham.

There was a young harlot of Clyde
Whose doctor cut open her hide.
  He misplaced her stitches
  And closed the wrong niches;
She now does her work on the side.

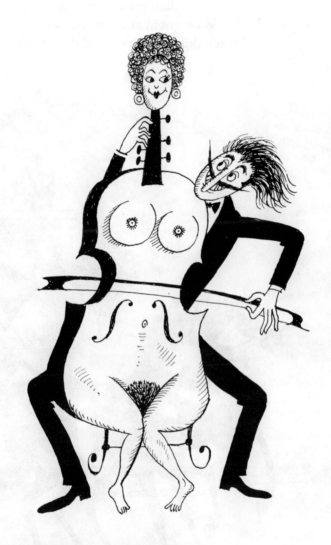

A young violinist from Rio
Was seduced by a lady named Cleo.
   As she took down her panties,
   She said, "No more *andantes*;
I want this *allegro con brio!*"

There was a young lady of Rhyll
In an omnibus was taken ill.
　　She called the conductor
　　Who got in and fucked her,
Which did her more good than a pill.

here was a young lady named
  Alice
Who peed in a Catholic chalice.
    She said, "I do this
    From a great need to piss,
And not from sectarian malice."

I wooed a stewed nude in Bermuda;
I was lewd, but my God! She was lewder.
    She said it was crude
    To be wooed in the nude —
I pursued her, subdued her, and screwed her!

There was a young lady named Wilde
Who kept herself undefiled
    By thinking of Jesus,
    Veneral diseases,
And the bother of having a child.

A sultan, inspecting his harem,
Said, "Eunuch, proceed to unbare 'em."
    Having seen the details,
    He issued long veils
And ordered the harem to wear 'em.
                 — Isaac Asimov

There was a young lady from Lynn
Who thought that to love was a sin;
    But when she was tight,
    It seemed quite all right,
So everyone filled her with gin.

here once was a warden of
Wadham,
Who approved of the folkways of Sodom,
 For a man might, he said,
 Have a very poor head,
But be a fine fellow, at bottom.

Said a woman, with open delight,
"My pubic hair's perfectly white.
 I admit there's a glare,
 But the fellows don't care.
They locate it more quickly at night."

     — Isaac Asimov

A wanton young lady at Wimley,
Reproached for not acting more primly,
 Answered, "Heavens above!
 I know sex isn't love,
But it's such an attractive facsimile."

A worried young man from Stamboul
Discovered red spots on his tool.
    Said the doctor, a cynic,
      "Get out of my clinic!
Just wipe off the lipstick, you fool."

61

 pious old lady of Brewster
Forgave all who'd ever abewster,
    But flew in a rage
    Time would not assuage
When she thought of the cad who'd refewster.
                — John Ciardi

Said Wilma, "Last week I believed
I had slipped and had somehow conceived.
    My prayers were myriad,
    Then I got my period,
And now for a while, I'm reprieved."
                — Isaac Asimov

She begged and she pleaded for more.
I said, "We've already had four,
    And I'm sure that you've heard,
    Though it's somewhat absurd,
That Eros spelt backwards is sorE."

There were three ladies from Huxham
And whenever we meets 'em we fucks 'em;
   And when that game grows stale,
   We sits on a rail
And pulls out our pricks and they sucks 'em.

There was a young man from St. John's,
Who wanted to bugger the swans.
    But the loyal hall-porter
    Said, "Pray, take my daughter,
Them birds are reserved for the Dons."

A salvation lassie named Claire
Was having her first love affair.
 As she climed into bed
 She reverently said,
"I wish to be opened with prayer."

The first troops under Spanish command
To set foot on Floridian sand
 Found a Seminole maid
 Who took trinkets in trade
And gave them the lay of the land.
    — John Ciardi

There was once a Duchess of Bruges
Whose cunt was incredibly huge.
 Said the Duke to his dame,
 As he thunderously came,
"Mon Dieu! Après moi, le Deluge!"

In the Garden of Eden lay Adam,
Amusing himself with his madam.
   He chuckled with mirth
   For on all this earth,
There were only two balls, and he had 'em.

A mathematician named Hall
Has a hexahedronical ball,
    And the cube of its weight
    Times his pecker, plus eight,
Is his phone number — give him a call!

A shiftless young fellow of Ghent
Had his wife screw the landlord for rent,
    But as she grew older
    The landlord grew colder
And now they live out in a tent.

The new cinematic emporium
Is not just a super-sensorium
    But a highly effectual
    Heterosexual
Mutual masturbatorium.

A colonial girl, sweet and sainted,
Was by war-striped young Indians tainted.
   Later, asked of the ravages,
   She said of the savages,
"They aren't as bad as they're painted."
             — Isaac Asimov

here was a young sailor from
Brighton
Who remarked to his girl, "You're a tight one."
    She replied, "'Pon my soul,
    You're in the wrong hole;
There's plenty of room in the right one."

To his bride, said young Galahad, "Kiddo,
Let's screw in each room, beach, and meadow,
    Every day, every night,
    In the dark, in the light."
And they tried it, and now she's a widow.
                              — Isaac Asimov

There was a young fellow of Sidney
Who, with women and wine, ruined his kidney.
    He screwed and he boozed,
    And his innards all oozed,
But he had a good time of it, didn't he?

There was a young girl from Dundee
Who was raped by an ape in a tree.
 The result was most horrid —
 All ass and no forehead,
Three balls and a purple goatee.

There was a young lady named Prentice,
Who had an affair with a dentist.
    To make the thing easier,
    He used anaesthesia
And diddled her, *non compis mentis.*

real estate man's imperfections
As a lover, caused female rejections.
    "I'm deflated," he moaned.
    "They're errogenous zoned,
But only for high-rise erections!"

There was a young woman named Melanie
Who was asked by a man, "Do you sell any?"
    She replied, "No, siree,
    I give it for free;
To sell it, dear sir, is a felony."
          — Isaac Asimov

An old maid in the land of Aloha
Got wrapped in the coils of a boa;
    And as the snake squeezed,
    The old maid, not displeased,
Cried, "Darling! I love it! Samoa!"

There was a young fellow from Kent
Whose prick was so long that it bent.
    To save himself trouble,
    He put it in double
And instead of coming, he went.

n elderly sage of B'nai B'rith
Told his friend he was quite full of pith.
    This could mean "full of fact"
    And "with meaning compact,"
But not when you're lithping like thith.
                 — Isaac Asimov

Over beer in a dimly lit bar,
I was puffing a ten-cent cigar,
    When a girl of a sort
    Said, "You look like a sport."
And my wife, in the shadows, said "Ha!"
                 — John Ciardi

A young polo-player of Berkeley
Made love to his sweetheart berserkly.
    In the midst of each chukker
    He would break off and fuck her
Horizontally, laterally, and verkeley.

A lovesick sky-diver named Sherm
Bailed out with his prick long and firm.
    Two jerks and a spasm
    Produced an orgasm,
And he spelled out, "I love you," in sperm.
                    — Isaac Asimov

wo dykes from the far Adriatic,
Deciding to be more pragmatic,
 Have switched from mere handling
 To mutual candling.
The result is, they're waxing ecstatic.

The girls who frequent picture-palaces
Set no store by psychoanalysis.
 Indeed, they're annoyed
 By the great Dr. Freud,
And they cling to their long-standing fallacies.
        (phalluses?)

There was a young laundress named Wrangle
Whose tits tilted up at an angle.
 "They may tickle my chin,"
 She said, with a grin,
"But at least they keep out of the mangle."

There was a young girl from Decatur
Who was fucked by an old alligator.
   No one ever knew
   How she relished that screw
For after he fucked her, he ate her.

Hitler had only one ball.
Goering had two, but 'twere small.
    And then there was Himmler
    Who had something sim'lar
But Goebbels had no balls at all.

here was a young man of
    La Jolla
Who kept screwing his wife in the folla.
      Those who passed by would mumble
      Or stub toes or stumble
But the folla was where he'd enjolla.
             — Isaac Asimov

Now what in the world shall we dioux
With the bloody and murderous Sioux,
      Who some time ago
      Took an arrow and bow
And raised such a hellabelioux?
             — Eugene Field

There was a young lady of Louth
Who returned from a trip to the South.
      Her papa said, "Nelly,
      There's more in your belly
Than ever went in by your mouth."

A Chinese lover, so slick,
Had a tool that was hard, long, and thick.
    When girls he would sclew,
    They sure liked to view
This Chinaman's big, blick-red plick.

There was a young girl from Hoboken
Who claimed that her hymen was broken
    From riding a bike
    On a cobblestone pike,
But it really was broken from pokin'.

There was an old bugger of Como
Who suddenly cried: "Ecce homo!"
   He traced his man down
    To the heart of the town,
And gobbled him off in the Duomo.

There was a young caveman named Ug
Who stuck his plug in a jug.
    Said Ug with a shrug,
    As he gave it a tug:
"Now ain't this a hell of a fug?"

here was a young woman from Wantage
Of whom the town clerk took advantage.
    Said the county surveyor,
    "Of course you must pay her;
You've altered the line of her frontage."

Said a woman from old San José,
To her lover, embarrassed, "Oh, say,
    This vagina of mine
    You say is like wine —
But today, I'm afraid, it's rosé."
        — Isaac Asimov

In the soap operas heard in Gomorrah,
The heroine wakes up in horror
    To find that a prick
    Nearly three inches thick
Is half up her — tune in tomorrow.

And then there's a story that's fraught
With disaster — of balls that got caught,
   When a chap took a crap
   In the woods, and a trap
Underneath — Oh! I can't bear the thought!

composer named Bela Bartok
Strung violin strings to his cock.
    He could play anything,
    From "God Save the King,"
To Johann Sebastian Bach.

There was a young lady of Michigan
Who said, "Damn it! I've got the itch again."
    Said her mother: "That's strange,
    I'm surprised it ain't mange,
If you've slept with that son of a bitch again."

At a gay bar, two young men inspected
Some girls whom they promptly rejected.
    In blank ennui,
    It was easy to see
They were totally other-directed.
                 — John Ciardi

A rapist's convicted and hence is
Executed for all his offenses.
   Thereafter, indeed,
    His victims agreed
That the man was well-hung in both senses.
       — Isaac Asimov

waitress on day-shift at
Schraffts
Has a couple of interesting craffts.
     She's exceedingly able
     At upsetting the table
And screwing in dumb waiter schaffts.

There was a young fellow from Boston
Who rode around in an Austin.
     There was room for his ass
     And a gallon of gas,
But his balls hung outside — and he lost 'em.

One semester, a young prof named Innis
Taught two hundred coeds what sin is.
     Not bad, I acknowledge,
     For a small country college,
But not worth recording in Guinness.
                              — John Ciardi

There was a young lady of Exeter,
So pretty that men craned their necks at her.
    One was even so brave
    As to take out and wave
The distinguishing mark of his sex at her.

"'Tis my custom," said dear Lady Norris,
"To beg lifts from the drivers of lorries.
    When they get out to piss,
    I see things I miss
At the wheel of my two-seater Morris."

here was a young lady named
  Jansen,
Whose Ma said, "I don't mind romancin'.
    You're young. Have your fling.
    But remember one thing:
When you stay out all night, keep on dancin'."
                                    — John Ciardi

The Duchess once asked, with a wink:
"Pray, tell me, Sir, why do farts stink?"
    I promptly replied
    With a grin very wide:
"For the benefit of the deaf, I think."

There was a young man from Cape Horn
Who wished he had never been born.
    And he wouldn't have been
    If his father had seen
That the end of the rubber was torn.

A vice, both obscure and unsavory,
Kept the Bishop of Chester in slavery.
'Midst terrible howls
He deflowered young owls,
In his crypt, fitted out as an aviary.

A n agreeable girl named
    Miss Doves
Likes to jack off the young men she loves.
        She will use her bare fist
        If the fellows insist,
But she really prefers to wear gloves.

There was a young woman named Suzie
Who was not much inclined to be choosy
        So that after a day
        Of intensive sex play
She was apt to remark, "Say, just who's he?"
                        — Isaac Asimov

With Robert, her boyfriend, Miss Cobb
Would nod, when engaged in a job.
        It was wrongfully said
        She was bobbing her head
When she really was heading her Bob.

To his lifestyle, she was unreconciled —
The mama of poor Oscar Wilde.
    "Do try to be hetero —
    Strong, brave, etcetro.
By young boys, don't get so beguiled!"

Young Dante Gabriel Rosetti
Was shagging a young lass named Betty.
    While her he bestrode,
    He composed a fine ode,
Then got up and ate some spaghetti.

There was a young lady of Dee
Who went down to the river to pee.
    A man in a punt
    Put his hand on her cunt,
And God! How I wish it was me.

There was a young man from Dumfries
Who said to his girl, "If you please,
    It would give me great bliss
    If, while playing with this,
You would pay some attention to these."

T here was a young farm girl
named Sutton
Who said, as she carved up the mutton,
    "My father preferred
    Screwing sheep from the herd.
This is one of his children I'm cuttin'."

A young nun who made notes in her diary
That were terribly torrid and fiery,
    Once left it behind
    For her abbess to find.
Now she isn't allowed in the priory.
               — Isaac Asimov

A geneticist living in Delft
Scientifically played with himself,
    And when he was done,
    He labeled it, "Son,"
And filed him away on a shelf.

There was a young lady of Wohl's Hill
Who sat herself down on a mole's hill.
   The resident mole
    Stuck his head up her hole.
The lady's all right, but the mole's ill.

f intercourse gives you
thrombosis,
While continence causes neurosis,
I prefer to expire
Fulfilling desire
Than to live in a state of psychosis.

"It's my code," said a mailman named Drew,
"To unzip, then deliver a screw.
If virgins, when nervous,
Resist postal service,
I explain that the male must go through."

A sensitive lady from Worcester,
At a ball, met a fellow who gorcester;
A lecherous guy
With blood in his eye,
So she ducked out before he sedorcester.

There was a young yokel named Spence,
Who was dumb and exceedingly dense.
To his girl, he said, "Where is
Your damn mons veneris?
I'm lost 'tween your odds and your ends."

here was a young girl named
Ann Heuser
Who said that no man could surprise her.
　　But Pabst took a chance,
　　Found a Schlitz in her pants,
And now she is sadder Budweiser.

Winter is here with a grouch;
The time when you sneeze and you slouch;
　　You can't take your women
　　Canoein' or swimmin'
But a lot can be done on a couch.

There was a young fellow from Yale
Whose face was exceedingly pale.
　　He spent his vacation
　　In self-masturbation
Because of the high price of tail.

The fat Prince of Wales, poor old Edward,
Preferred not to look at all bedward,
 For, with girls in the sack,
 He hadn't the knack.
His member was just so much deadwood.

When he wooed fair Lady Regina,
And graciously wined her and dined her,
   The stout grenadier
    Got terribly near —
But finally missed her vagina!

There was a young lady of Eton
Whose figure had plenty of meat on.
    She said, "Marry me, dear,
    And you'll find that my rear
Is a nice place to warm your cold feet on."

There was a young lady of Norway
Who hung by her toes in a doorway.
    She said to her beau:
    "Just look at me, Joe,
I think I've discovered one more way."

here was an old rake from
Stamboul,
Felt his ardor grow suddenly cool.
No lack of affection
Reduced his erection,
But his zipper got caught in his tool.

There was a young student named Jones
Who'd reduce any maiden to groans
By his wonderful knowledge
Acquired in college,
Of nineteen erogenous zones.

"Since my sex is bisex," said Casey,
"I've chosen a city that's racy.
With its either-or zest,
I get letters addressed
To Washington, D.C. or A.C."

There was a young lady from Twickenham
Who thought men had not enough prick in 'em.
 On her knees every day,
 To God she would pray,
To lengthen and strengthen and thicken 'em.

here was a young woman
   named Vicki
Who said, "I don't want to be picky.
      If, in five hours or so
      As you say, you must go,
At least we'll have time for a quicky."
                              — Isaac Asimov

When asked to do something salacious,
She answered, "Of course not! Good gracious!"
      But the sight of his tool
      So induced her to drool
That her view, in the end, was fellatious.

There was a young lady named Mabel
Who said, "I don't think that I'm able;
      But I'm willing to try,
      So where shall I lie?
On the bed, on the floor, or the table?"

There was a mad monk called Rasputin
Whose prowess was not for disputin'.
    His wondrous czassotzkys
    Gave women the hottskis —
Tsarinas and all, you're damn tootin'!

The practice that's known as minette
Was cherished by fair Juliet.
    She'd say to him, "Blow me, oh
    My dearest Romeo."
Whenever her lover she met.

f you're speaking of actions
  immoral,
Then how about giving the laurel
    To doughty Queen Esther,
    No three men could best her —
One fore, one aft, and one oral.

Said a lecherous fellow named Shea,
When his prick wouldn't rise for a lay,
    "You must seize it and squeeze it
    And tease it and please it,
For Rome wasn't built in a day."

"My back aches. My penis is sore.
I simply can't screw any more.
    I'm dripping with sweat,
    You haven't come yet;
And, my God! It's a quarter to four!"

There was a young nun from Siberia
Endowed with a virgin interior,
    Until an old monk
    Jumped into her bunk,
And now she's Mother Superior.

There was a young girl from Ostend
Who her maidenhead tried to defend,
    But a Chasseur d'Afrique
    Inserted his prick
And taught that ex-maid how to spend.

 got into bed with Dolores
And her diaphragm proved to be porous.
    The result of our sins
    Was a fine pair of twins;
Now the birth control people abhor us.
                       — Isaac Asimov

There was a young lady named Hall,
Wore a newspaper dress to a ball.
    The dress caught on fire
    And burned her entire
Front page, sporting section, and all.

A good-looking lass named Regina
Had teeth in her little vagina.
    When a man with her mated,
    He soon was castrated
While she sighed, "Oh well, and good-bye now!"

There was a young lady named Ransom,
Who was rogered three times in a hansom.
  When she cried out for more,
  A voice from the floor
Said, "My name is Simpson, not Sampson."

FRDOES

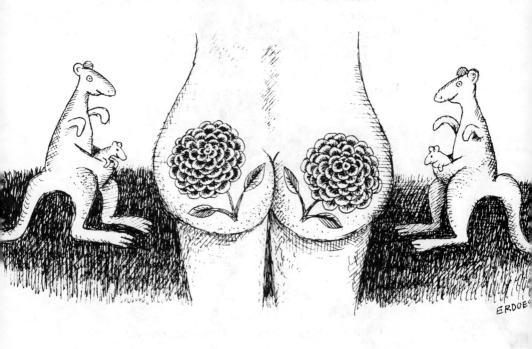

There was a young man from Australia
Who painted his ass like a dahlia.
    The color was fine
    And the drawing divine,
But the smell — that was a big failure.

 certain hard-working young hooker
Was such an enchanting good-looker,
    There were fights 'mongst the fuzz
    Over whose turn it was
To pinch her and frisk her and book her.
               — Isaac Asimov

Take the case of a lady named Frost,
Whose organ is three feet acrost.
    It's the best part of valor
    To bugger the gal, or
One's apt to fall in and get lost.

"It's dull in Duluth, Minnesota.
Of spirit, there's not an iota —"
    Complained Alice to Joe,
    Who tried not to show
That he yawned in her snatch as he blowed her.

A lady, while dining in Crewe,
Found an elephant's whang in her stew.
  Said the waiter, "Don't shout,
  And don't wave it about,
Or the others will all want one too."

There was an old Bishop of Dee
Who, alas, could no longer pee.
He said, "Pax Vobiscum!
    Why doesn't der piss cum?
It must be the old gonorrhea!"

here was a young lady from
Putney
Who was given to sexual gluttony.
 Warned a pious old duffer,
 "Your morals will suffer."
"That's what you think," she said. "I ain't gutney."
      — John Ciardi

There was a young lady named Hilda
Who went driving, one night, with a builder.
 He said that he should,
 That he could and he would
And he did and he pretty near killda.

While the bill was debated, Miss Snyder
Had a senator thrusting inside her.
 To a knock on the door,
 He replied from the floor,
"Go away, I'm inserting a rider."

There was a young lady of Bude,
Who walked around practically nude.
    A stroller said, "Whattum
      Magnificent bottom!"
And slapped it as hard as he could.

A lady, removing her scanties,
Heard them crackle electrical chanties.
Said her husband, "My dear,
I very much fear
You suffer from amps in your panties."

A young woman married in Chester,
Her mother, she kissed her and blessed her.
    Says she, "You're in luck,
    He's a stunning good fuck,
For I've had him myself down in Leicester."

There was a young man from the coast
Who had an affair with a ghost.
    At the height of orgasm,
    This female phantasm
Said, "I think I can feel it — almost!"

gentleman living in Fife
Made love to the corpse of his wife.
    "How could I know, Judge?
    She was cold, did not budge —
Just the same as she'd acted in life."

There was a young couple from Florida
Whose passion grew steadily torrider.
    They were planning to sin
    In a room in an inn
Who can wait? So they screwed in the corridor.
                 — Isaac Asimov

A delighted incredulous bride
Remarked to the groom by her side:
    "I never could quite
    Believe till tonight
Our anatomies would coincide."

An Olympian lecher was Zeus,
Always playing around fast and loose,
With one hand in the bodice
Of some likely young goddess
And the other preparing to goose.
— Isaac Asimov

There was a young lady in Natchez
Who fell in some nettle-wood patches.
    She sits in her room
    With her bare little moon
And scratches and scratches and scratches.

And there was young Lady Matthias,
Whose bloomers were cut on the bias,
    With an opening behind
      To let out the wind,
And to let the boys in once or twias.

t his wedding, a bridegroom named Crusoe
Was embarrassed to find his prick grew so.
    His eager young bride
    Pulled him quickly astride
And was screwed while still wearing her trousseau.

            —Isaac Asimov

To the ancient Greek writer, Herodotus,
Said a pretty young thing, "My, how hard it is."
    Said he, "Do you fear
    I will hurt you, my dear?"
And she said, "Are you crazy? Thank God, it is."

            —Isaac Asimov

Call the study of figures "statistics,"
And the study of language "linguistics,"
    But it's clear that one errs
    When one loosely avers
That the study of balling's "ballistics."

At the movies, a young girl named Lynn
Wet her pants watching brash Errol Flynn.
    Lugosi the vampire
    Made them even damper.
They dried up, though, with Rin-tin-tin.

He marched to the sound of the flute,
And they taught him some firearms to shoot.
    "You're right on the target,"
      Said sweet girlfriend, Margaret,
"And your musket is awfully cute!"

A pansy who lived in Khartoum
Took a lesbian up to his room,
    And they argued all night
    Over who had the right
To do what and with which and to whom.
                   —Norman Douglas

Rosalina, a pretty young lass,
Had a truly magnificent ass:
    Not rounded and pink
    As you possibly think—
It was gray, had long ears, and ate grass.

There was a young girl from Penn State
Who stuttered when out on a date.
    By the time she cried "S-s-s-stop!"
    Or called for a c-c-c-cop,
It was often a wee bit too late.

Old Louis Quatorze was hot stuff.
He tired of that game, Blindman's Buff —
    Upended his mistress,
        Kissed hers while she kissed his,
And thus taught the world *soixante-neuf*.

here was a young fellow
named Spiegel
Who had an affair with a seagull—
    What's worse, do you see,
    It wasn't a she
But a he-gull—and *that* is illegal.
             —John Ciardi

Said an ovum one night to a sperm,
"You're a very attractive young germ.
    Come join me, my sweet,
    Let our nuclei meet
And in nine months, we'll both come to term.
             —Isaac Asimov

There was a young lady of Dover
Whose passion was such that it drove her
    To shout, when I came,
    "Oh dear, what a shame!
Well, now we shall have to start over!"

There was an old abbess quite shocked
To find nuns where the candles were locked.
    Said the abbess: "You nuns
    Should behave more like guns
And never go off till you're cocked."

Cleopatra's a cute little minx,
With a sex life that's loaded with kinks.
Marcus A. she would steer amid
The palms and Great Pyramid
And they'd screw on the head of the sphinx.
—Isaac Asimov

here was a young coed from
   Norwood
Whose ways were provokingly forward.
    Said her mother, "My dear,
    You wiggle, I fear,
Your posterior the way that a whore would."

There was a young lady who lay
With her legs wide apart in the hay,
    Then, calling the ploughman,
    She said, "Do it now, man!
Don't wait till your hair has turned gray!"

Said a learned old man of Brabant,
"The instinct, my dear, is extant:
    The extension's extinct.
    Or to be more succinct:
I would if I could, but I can't."
                — John Ciardi

It always delights me at Hanks
To walk up the old river banks.
    One time in the grass,
    I stepped on an ass
And heard a young girl murmur, "Thanks!"

here was a young fellow called
Skinner
Who took a young lady to dinner;
     At half past nine
     They sat down to dine
And by quarter to ten, he was in her.

There was a young girl from Sofia
Who succumbed to her lover's desire.
     She said, "It's a sin,
     But now that it's in,
Could you shove it a few inches higher?"

On a maiden, a man once begat
Male triplets named Nat, Pat, and Tat.
     It was fun in the breeding,
     But hell in the feeding.
She hadn't a spare tit for Tat.

While having a bit of romance,
Jane put a hand in Joe's pants.
In defying convention
And offering attention
She made his limp member a lance.

The Homeric young fighter, Achilles,
Was great with the fair Trojan fillies,
    But Paris said, "We'll
    Just aim at his heel."
Now Achilles is pushing up lilies.
                    —Isaac Asimov

widow, whose singular vice
Was to keep her late husband on ice,
　　Said, "It's been hard since I lost him—
　　I'll never defrost him!
Cold comfort, but cheap at the price."

An amorous maiden antique
Locked a man in her house for a week;
　　He entered her door
　　With a shout and a roar
But his exit was marked with a squeak.

There was a young man from Kildare
Who was having a girl on the stair.
　　At the sixty-third stroke
　　The bannister broke
So he finished her off in mid-air.

There was a young lady at sea
Who complained that it hurt her to pee.
    Said the brawny old mate:
    "That accounts for the state
Of the cook and the captain and me."

About Richard Erdoes...

Originally from Vienna, Richard Erdoes describes himself as an old, somewhat wrinkled artist, and a young budding writer. Having studied at the art academies of Vienna and Paris, he wrote and illustrated satiric articles making fun of the Nazis, who did not appreciate his humor. When he also printed an underground newspaper after Hitler's rise to power, he had a price on his head and fled—first to Paris, then to London, ending up, to his great surprise, in the United States. He became a well-known magazine and book illustrator receiving numerous prizes and awards from the New York Art Director's Club, the American Institute for Graphic Arts, and the Society of Illustrators.

At *LIFE* Magazine, he met his wife of forty years, Jean, a fellow artist. They have two sons, one daughter, and two grandchildren. An enthusiastic traveler, camper, and skier, Erdoes soon discovered the American West which has held him spellbound ever since. The Erdoes family formed strong and lasting friendships with native Americans and became deeply involved in the struggle for Indian Civil Rights. Their New York apartment was for many years known as "Sioux East," and it was a Sioux medicine man who turned Erdoes, the artist, into a writer, by telling him, over and over again: "My medicine tells me that you will do my book." Erdoes did, and since then, has had over a dozen books published, many of them on Indian life and western history. He has also illustrated numerous books, both adult and juvenile. Spending most of his time in Santa Fe, he now divides his time evenly between painting and writing.

About Isaac Asimov...

One of the most distinguished and prolific authors of our time, Isaac Asimov will not need much introducing to our readers. A graduate of Columbia University with a Ph.D. in Chemistry, Isaac Asimov is a professor of Chemistry at Boston University School of Medicine. At the time of going to press, a staggering two hundred and ninety-seven books by Isaac Asimov have been published, but he has assured us that the number will have reached three hundred by the time this book reaches the stores. These titles include an impressive range of fiction, science-fiction, books for children, books on science, space, the solar system, mathematics, and most germane to this context—five volumes of original limericks.